MELISSA ANDREOTTI

illustrated by
LIANA CHEN

SOMETIMES I'M ME

a book for children with
PANS/PANDAS
and their friends

Copyright © 2025 by Melissa Andreotti

A book aimed at children and friends of those with Paediatric Acute-onset Neuropsychiatric Syndrome / Paediatric Autoimmune Neuropsychiatric Disorder Associated with Streptococcus (PANS/ PANDAS).

All rights reserved, including the right to reproduce this book or portions thereof in any form whatsoever.

Publisher:
Inspiring Publishers
PO Box 159, Calwell, ACT 2905, Australia.
Phone: 61-(0) 2 6291-2904
http://australianselfpublishinggroup.com

A catalogue record for this book is available from the National Library of Australia

National Library of Australia Prepublication Data Service

Author: Melissa Andreotti

Title: **SOMETIMES I'M ME**

ISBN: 978-1-923449-79-4 (print)
ISBN: 978-1-923449-80-0 (eBook)

This book was written when there wasn't anything available to explain PANS/PANDAS to my young son's friends who had been on the receiving end of some of his symptoms. I wanted a child friendly way to explain what was going on for my son in an easy to understand and non-threatening way. I wanted to explain that sometimes he is the 'real' version of himself that we all love, and other times he is not- but please hang in there, he'll be back soon. That's how 'Sometimes I'm Me' came about. I hope this book can help those families living with this devastating condition in some small way.

This book is dedicated to my beautiful son. You are the 'best boy in forever' and I will never stop fighting for you. Mum xx

Sometimes I'm me. I'm healthy and I act just like myself. I am kind, silly, generous and funny.

When I'm the real me, I have control over my body and I don't usually say mean things or do strange things. I love playing with my friends and I feel happy most of the time.

But sometimes, usually after I'm sick,
alien pandas break into my brain and stop it
from working properly. They try to control me.

They trick me into saying things that are
mean and rude, even to people I like.

I try to overpower them but sometimes they win.
It can make my friends feel hurt and sad when
I say and do mean things. I really am sorry,
and I don't mean them at all.

They also make my body do strange things like pee a lot, sniff my hands and make strange or loud noises. I may even look a bit different and might seem more tired, moody and cross.

Sometimes they trick me into worrying about things that I normally wouldn't be worried about, like being away from my mum. Or they trick me into thinking that food has poison in it, or that there is a monster hiding in my room. Or that I need to do things a certain way or something bad might happen. It can be really confusing and scary.

I really hate these alien pandas and wish they didn't break into my brain.

They make me do things I don't want to do and I can't control it!

My doctors, mum and dad are trying really hard to stop the alien pandas from breaking into my brain and I try to stay as healthy as possible.

I have to make sure I eat healthy and look after my body.

Being a friend to someone who has
alien pandas invade them is really hard.

If you ever notice I'm acting different,
or you think the alien pandas might be controlling me,
you can let an adult you trust know.

It's okay to be upset with me or take a break away from me when the alien pandas are in control. I will try to fight them off as quickly as possible, so I can go back to being me again.

Thank you for being so patient with me
and for being such a great friend.
It means the world to me!

About PANS/PANDAS

PANS ("Paediatric Acute-onset Neuropsychiatric Syndrome") is a clinically defined disorder characterised by the sudden onset of obsessive-compulsive symptoms or eating restrictions, concomitant with acute behavioural regression in at least two designated domains. Comorbid PANS symptoms may include: anxiety, sensory amplification or motor abnormalities, behavioral regression, deterioration in school performance, mood disorder, urinary symptoms and/or sleep disturbances.

PANS does not require a known trigger, although it is believed to be triggered by one or more pathogens."

PANDAS ("Paediatric Autoimmune Neuropsychiatric Disorders Associated with Streptococcal Infections") is a subset of PANS and was first reported by a team at the National Institute of Mental Health (part of NIH) in 1998. PANDAS has 5 distinct criteria for diagnosis, including abrupt "overnight" OCD or dramatic, disabling tics; a relapsing-remitting, episodic symptom course; young age at onset (average of 6–7 years); presence of neurologic abnormalities; and temporal association between symptom onset and Group A strep (GAS) infection. The 5 criteria usually are accompanied by similar comorbid symptoms as found in PANS."

(Source: PANDAS Physician Network, pandasppn.org/what-are-pans-pandas/, March 2025)

For more information please visit the following websites:

- www.pandasppn.org
- aspire.care
- pandasnetwork.org
- pansaustralia.com
- panspandasuk.org

About the Author

 Melissa Andreotti is a mother and Occupational Therapist who studied and works in Melbourne, Australia in various settings including hospital and community. When her son was faced with unexplained psychiatric and neurological challenges, she and her husband turned to their General Practitioner who, amazingly, had heard of and treated other children with PANS. Upon initial treatment, Mel recalled a dramatic improvement in her son and had felt like she had met the 'real' him for the first time. As time went on and relapses were regular, Mel wanted a way to spread awareness to others and to explain to her son's friends what was going on for him in a child-friendly way. That's how 'Sometimes I'm Me' came about.

Mel is a fierce advocate for children's rights and PANS/PANDAS awareness and is passionate about making a difference to the families affected by this difficult condition.

About the Illustrator

Liana Chen lives on the sunny Hibiscus Coast of Auckland, New Zealand, and is a proud mother to three fun-loving boys (Ryan, Tommy, and Jack).

With a decade-long background in physio-therapy, it was motherhood that truly opened Liana's eyes (and heart) to the magical, complex world of children—especially those who experience the world a little differently. Through a period of personal rediscovery, Liana uncovered a long-lost love for art and story telling—two things she now uses to connect, comfort, and celebrate children just as they are.

Liana hopes her illustrations will help to bring a little magic, kindness, and understanding to wherever it's needed most."

www.ingramcontent.com/pod-product-compliance
Lightning Source LLC
Chambersburg PA
CBHW041121070526
44584CB00002B/233